Goddess of the Whole Self

poems by

Sherrie Fernandez-Williams

Finishing Line Press
Georgetown, Kentucky

Goddess
of the Whole Self

Copyright © 2023 by Sherrie Fernandez-Williams
ISBN 979-8-88838-296-7 First Edition
All rights reserved under International and Pan-American Copyright Conventions. No part of this book may be reproduced in any manner whatsoever without written permission from the publisher, except in the case of brief quotations embodied in critical articles and reviews.

Publisher: Leah Huete de Maines
Editor: Christen Kincaid
Cover Art: Sherrie Fernandez-Williams
Author Photo: Anna Min of Min Enterprises
Cover Design: Elizabeth Maines McCleavy

Order online: www.finishinglinepress.com
also available on amazon.com

Author inquiries and mail orders:
Finishing Line Press
P. O. Box 1626
Georgetown, Kentucky 40324
U. S. A.

Table of Contents

Goddess of resistance
May the Circle 1
how she keeps...2
Crave..3
The Crossing 6
Homeland, Like the Girl Who Sang Soweto, After June Jordan 7
Homage..9
Hot Tea 11
acknowledgments 13
For John Robert 15

Goddess of bewilderment
There isn't a Simple Answer..................................19
the son and the father. Part 1. 24
the son and the father. Part 2. 25
sparrow 27
Juanita 29

Goddess of the damned
She be like, damn! 33
Wind Dream...34
Night Perceptions...35
Nerves 38
no peace 40
Hunger 42
Goddess of the middle
   i. in the middle..47
   ii. in the middle...49
   iii. in the middle 51
   iv. in the middle..53

Goddess of the integrating lesbian
with no disrespect to officer quinn 57
carried 58
Like You Mean it 60
Overflow 65
Breath 69
Writing Prompt from Mimi Imuro Van Ausdall 71
Goddess of the Integrated Lesbian 72

Maybe when I wake up in the middle of the night
I should go downstairs
dump the refrigerator contents on the floor
and stand there in the middle of the spilled milk
and wasted butter spread beneath my dirty feet
writing poems
writing poems
maybe I just need to love myself myself and
anyway
I'm working on it.

—June Jordan

Preface

> *Some say God is a spirit, a force, an ultimate reality. Ask seven people what all of that means, and you'll get seven different answers. So what is God? Just another name for whatever makes you feel special and protected*
> —Lauren Olamina from Octavia Butler's *Parable of the Sower*

I find comfort in the idea of Goddess, a Goddess who doesn't necessarily exist to protect me but will protect me when necessary; a source of wisdom, helping me discover my special.

This Goddess is quiet, most present in stillness.

This Goddess encourages me to progress but accept my limitations—Strive but not at the expense of anyone's well-being, including mine.

This Goddess knows how I hurt even though invisible wounds are nearly impossible to describe. This Goddess needs no explanation because they hurt in similar ways. This Goddess relates.

This Goddess knows the history of my DNA, each marker, and each person who provided me with that marker. They remind me to invite helpful ancestors to participate. I would not be without them.

This Goddess knows what's been handed to me, what's been hurled at me, and what I've claimed for myself.

This Goddess reminds me the interior isn't everything. There is a world outside—wrestle with it. It cannot be escaped. Although I do not always feel safe as a black, queer person, who values harmony, this Goddess offers strategies for living in a hostile world. They remind me I am one of many residents. We've been brought up together in this era, like family. Sometimes family can be hard to understand.

This Goddess understands when I say I feel deeply rooted and unrooted at the same time. There is bravery in being unrooted or uprooted from what you once believed. Be rooted in this.

Goddess of resistance

May the Circle

Our Mothers who art in heaven,
who will save this motherfucker
when he wakes in his own vomit.

We came to mist-freshened earth
to dig in and plant toes
until they are fully rooted,
to swallow disorienting carbon
then respire like Jesus saves, and the devil lies
and to rebuke him like the grandmothers
learned from their grandmothers
to rebuke him like Cora taught Rosa
in the name of her granddaughter, my mother,
in the name of our prophets,
like Ms. June Jordan, we are
Black and alive and looking back at you.

in the name of Ochún, the youngest of the saints,
in the name of the grownup baby girl wanting to
recall the day before this pissy-punk
carved his mug onto her frontal lobe
along with other recollections: his weight, for example,
his hand on her mouth, his laughter, her struggle
to survive beyond that day, that one small room, to become,
in the name of an active citizen with an enriched mind,
and one day, a sharer of insights,
in the name of a woman
happy to make love when that is what she desires,
in the name of a decision maker, a mother, maybe, someday,
and someday, maybe, a grandmother herself.
in the name of an ancestor willing to return, when might is needed
because she will be The General.

Puking may endure for a night, but sobriety comes
when a root woman looks you dead in the eyes.

In the morning, no wind will split these thick ass trunks.
Branch locked to branch, a multiplying assembly,
Goddesses descending, forest closing in.

how she keeps

she wonders how long before
her frame knows all it must
do is extend, bend, land; a shifting
of weight, a solid gait,
a privilege, a mechanism

motivated, first by curiosity,
then, a function of need
now, a matter of hope,
an inclination towards wholeness
an ordered self well cared for

reminding her to stay in motion,
a rhythm, a camel promenading,
across the saharan where we
all begin. tiny hair of the inner ear
bounces to *tinariwen*

she thinks of a taurug
woman of the desert,
the keeper of valuables,
her tent at the center.
free in love. one thousand
years of a people traced through her.
what does this knowing do
for this woman?

she wonders how long before her
own body knows it is the keeper
of treasures, and her immortal soul has
endless chances to get things right.

dune blues fill the empty places.
her limbs swing. her body
carries memory made and found;
friday night amusement-filled pop-ins,
her grandmother's immigration
records stored in a database.

she prints, punches, and places
history into a red binder purchased for
such findings. she wants to know joy.

extend, bend, land, a shifting of weight,
her state of mind, her way of being

fully integrated. full of intent.
tinariwen sings to her. As she hums,
sand spills from her fingers. her body,
her tent is the center, the keeper.

she believes as she walks.

a thousand miles from arid land,
she returns to this moment
shared with a silver lake, like nickel.
stands face to face with lemon yellow
and soft pink, murmuring life
in tall grasses, bringing her
to now. now, is what is real.

now, this body she will carry
forward among rhododendron.
now, she will breathe,
move deeper from belief to knowing,
and embolden all that is alive beneath
her skin. extend, bend, land a shifting
of weight. these buckeyes are like
spirits, not easily broken; she knows as she walks.

Crave

a crop
bound and dispersed

of distressed wombs now
buried or burnt
return often
to keep
eye on
the crop
they were

yanked from, and
the fig and
millet that
satiated them.

budding memory
crop like
tuberous root, a yam,
hybrid origin
of both forest
and savanna
downward into dahomey,

removed

to chop
crops of cane
to better someone's tea.

birthed babies also
hybrid of origin
one part haplogroup R1b,
darkened in their bodies

sail once more
to something new
yielded of
infected root

cropped out
but extant
sewing dust
air and faith
for food
and cropping up
everywhere
because they are
still hungry

The Crossing

We are building a viaduct
because we decided
this time,
we will not travel
underground, live in The Great Dismal,
drag our bodies through the marsh,
hide in the cattails.
In the plain view of daylight
above the gorge,
as high as Millau in France,
our railway.
Once we perfect the art of brickmaking,
you can decide how many are needed.
That woman over there, maybe she can
decide how many tons
our spillway can hold.
This old one with the braids
like a hive,
I hope she'll teach us about
steel.
She knows how to reduce
sulfur from iron to keep it strong.
Look at her hands.
Look at her crafted shoulders,
but do not touch without invitation.

Darlings, there is a job
for us too.
Ours might be the gathering kind.
Talkers sing like brave birds.
Poets plow the topsoil.
Dancers paint with perennials.

We will call all hands.
Hurting hands are beautiful.
Photographers shoot
for our annual day of remembrance.
We can alternate hosts. I'll sign up for that.
We have all agreed, no borders. No borders. No borders. No borders.

Homeland, Like the Girl Who Sang Soweto
after *A Song for Soweto* by June Jordan

Did you know Sister June told how they wanted that girl to swallow dust?
Instead, she puckered and kissed Soweto. *Homeland*, she said.
Sister June be coming around when I'm lost and walking in circles
Because this land has never been/has always been home.
Blessed are those who move in circles, for theirs is a purposeful rotation.

Spinning earth keeps the topsoil from being
swept into the atmosphere along with
rock, tree, clay, coast, ocean, all of us, and everything.
Blessed are those who spin, for they will plow our way forward.

Did you know Sister June told about the girl who drank water when they wanted to draw blood?
Strain cucumber in a mesh sieve, add cold water and a few cranberries, pour over
ice. Drink and serve the thirsty. Grief is a bitter kind of parched.
Blessed are those who thirst for righteousness, for they will soon be satisfied.

Now, imagine this, going home
like the girl who kissed Soweto and said *Homeland*:
Nigeria, Dahomey, Ghana, Spain,
England, Cameroon, Germany!
Wait! Nearly there.
Portugal, Senegal, Mali
The Southern Bantu Peoples
Ireland, Indigenous Americas
Norway,
Basque—
by way of the transatlantic, brought to Barbados, Cuba, Georgia, North Carolina by way of rape, at times, a toe from one people, a fingernail from another, an eyelash from another.

> *Blessed are those who are from here and there.*
> *Restless spirits may roam in the*
> *afterlife in search of that final rest.*

Did you know Sister June remembered the girl who was afraid that the Law would take her father?

We know well about the Law that taketh away and giveth no justice.
Sister June lays it down when I find myself unnaturally bent until the spine has a permanent curve.

Blessed are the meek, for their backs can carry twice their weight.

Sister June remembered the girl who stayed with her song. Homeland, she sang. Soweto.

What song shall I sing for hope in this present?
Blessed are those who tell the truth, for the devil will be shamed.

Sister June tells how they wanted that girl to crawl into her own grave, but she stood under the sun instead.
Blessed are those with a body to stand under the sun, for some bodies can no longer stand.

Blessed are
> *the demonstrators*
> *the agitators*
> *the highway invaders*
> *the bail arrangers*

Blessed are those who know they are, from the top of their sculls to the soles of their feet, sovereign.

Imagine this; my homeland is my body. I am at home in
my body, and the ground on which my body lives,
the ground on which my body builds, is blessed because of me.
Imagine that my body is my home, and my invocation.

I hear Sister June say, stop circling now. Stop spinning.
Blessed are those who are at home with themselves.

Homage

Following you sister into your room,
you are there beyond my imaginings.
The withering wood speaks back to me as I enter.
It tells me I am welcomed,
but not to disturb the souls
resting on the credenza or
burgundy leather chair
near the narrow window
sealed shut by time.

Spirits transferred onto stacks of paper,
you have made yourself present
and saved the lives of our dead
and resurrected even the living.

Not contorting, you aimed for greater aspirations
risking what we fear most, misunderstanding.
Building your own structure to store
evidence of your existence and ours,
Offering provocative critique of fundamental realities,
in other words, the lies some have told

Your candor upon white canvases,
keep us from being blanketed,
shoved into dank corners to choke on someone else's dust.

I stand in your room, not wanting to agitate the souls who have
found rest through your remembering of them.
You have given us all you had
and I dare not ask for more.

I only want to say thank you.
Thank you, Sister June, for a poem about my rights.
Thank you for our living dreams Lorraine,
for new dimensions, Octavia.
Thank you, Zora. We know our worth.
I am one of your Brown Girls, Paule.
Lucille, we will sail through this and that.

Gwendolyn, a hard city won't end us.
You whispered this in my ear, Ntozake.
Maya, how did you learn to love like that?
And Toni, I will follow you, sister,
out of and into the dark. Say when it is time.

And there are sisters who gather each month
to share our own selections
and grieve the loss of mothers, fathers, grandmothers
spouses, and, dear heavens, children,
reminding ourselves that laughter sends
delight from the brain to the hurting places.

We hale from across the strata,
across the country, and care less about who does
or does not love us. In the space we hold,
we shed enough love to soothe galaxies.
If our world listened
it would breathe easier.

Think of Thede and her funny friends,
celebrating at the mere sight of one another.
Who defends and who prosecutes loses relevance.
They are all in it for the same cause, after all.
The first to notice begins the
song. Then, all join the rhapsody.
It isn't important if anyone else gets it.
No one else is there to question.

Although our paths are not all the same,
although the stories are not all the same,
(we, of course, know the
dangers of thoughtless suppositions)
what we share is the ability to see each other,
and what we share are our foremothers
of verse and prose and foreknowing,
and what we share is our need to tell tales,
and what we share is our allegiance to
witnessing the ways we all pay homage.

Hot Tea

Young dignitary, emancipate your feet.
Stretch your back
across an acre embroidered
in African Moons.
You are like their seedlings
in need of water.

Young dignitary,
miles of highway know the
impression of your shoe
by heart. It is tender
at your core. The injured hum
their names. Faces soaked up by the cortex
for sight cannot be unseen
and the ground where they last stood
must absorb a life poured out.

Young dignitary, my daughter,
woman of the infantry, I was afraid
all those nights you broke the Governor's
curfew to cry out into the
Minneapolis night, while they shot
rubber bullets at you and shouted,
at you and your comrades,
threatened to light you all up if
you did not go home, and you did
not go home. And, I was wrong
for asking you to please go home, and as you know,
that wasn't the first time I have been wrong.

Young dignitaries, this agony, you haul
with all subtle movements
and speak at movements of
national proportions.
Voices shouting beyond their limits,
crescendos into whispers.
Hot chamomile with lemon and honey
will help. I have prepared this for you.

Sit as we remember our future. Rest
until you are well again to move us further.

acknowledgments

i acknowledge you
public housing
medicaid glasses to see the green chalkboard
measles, mumps, and rubella shots
at the department of public health
and penicillin for foot and mouth disease
and strep.
i acknowledge you
monthly check
parceled
to the housing authority,
phone company on willoughby street,
and for the intrepid sea, air & space museum school trips.
i acknowledge you
    food-stamps
    for canned stew and wonder bread
    free lunch, and, of course,
    free cheese
free homework help at dr. white community center
fresh air fun took black children to
the appalachian mountains
to be stared at by white children.
pell grants and
subsidized loans, i acknowledge you.
after decades, there's only 70k left to pay. but i pray all will be forgiven..soon.

acknowledging feeble consolations
not prizes
for the zealous commitment to break, hoard, control, misremember
for forty acres promised
for making enslavers whole instead
for the institutions funded through the buying and selling of our folk
and the economy that ran on what they produced.

no dollar amount,
can repair,
because how could it?
because ships and chains
because whips

lynchings
terror
the burning of towns
black wealth in ashes
dismembered communities
dissected by highways
and so-called urban "renewal."
because redlining
because incarceration en masse
because excessive force
because lead in drinking our water
because greed
and the attempt to erase everything,
erase culpability,
erase evidence of who benefitted
erase evidence of what we still endure

      and even as we reconstruct, and reconstruct again, and reevaluate and
                                    recover from destruction,
      and even as we reimagine life after displacement
      and even as we make visible what's been denied and misappropriated
      and even though there is no absolution for irreparable debts,

we will hear the best offer
bring some peace to old spirits
cool what smolders
expose the flame and the gas,
and bring those who light it to the altar of their god

for John Robert

Pick up the padding
that dims the sound.
Crazy-glue them to the walls
until there is no space left
to cover. Then, let it out.

His tongue could not be held,
not even in the chicken coup.
Son of two God-fearing who
asked him to please hold it in.

He was told it will come to pass
in heaven, the beloved community
he craved.

He, too, feared God
but did not fear
bloody Sundays.
He was not afraid
of the perilous business of
liberating lunch counters.
His own rap sheet of 45—
was the trouble he made for good

While the 45th, a swindler,
pecks at the vulnerable
and clucks absurdities
all the way to the bank.
That one is unworthy of
sharing a verse

with our young radical
turned elder statesmen,
equally joyful as he was abiding
to his purpose
who stepped out of the safety
with a tall carriage
with no haven or
helmet to protect him.

To the young
who represent,

and lay plans,
get souls to vanishing polls,
legislate against odiousness,

To the grandparents who endure
the muggy south,
risk heat stroke to exercise their will

To humanity who steps out
with a tall carriage
to face a contingency
that still chooses
mayhem,

John Robert's assignment
has fallen
into destined hands
imbued by
the young radical
turned esteemed elder statesmen.

Through all of us, he will never stop preaching to chickens.

Goddess of the bewildered

There is no simple answer

1.
Something almost remembered then pushed away
for a later date only to find its way into the body, dawdle there,
and hope to be recognized, assessed, sifted through for what good
it carries, then separated from its waste.

If left alone for too long, it splinters into the convolution
gray matter latching onto cells, weakening them.

Sometimes it arrives as a simple question while listening to gossip
radio, while not wanting to be bothered by anything too taxing,
like separating sewage from my cells while driving home from a hard day's
work.

The words link together, and I remove them like a chain from the bottom
of my belly, straight out of my mouth.

"What do I do with the men?"

2.
I know what the question means.

I love Daddy. He was forty when I was born. When I turned forty,
I was the adult daughter. Tenacious. Never falling apart
for too long, anyway, since enacting my three-day rule.
Three days to be dumbfounded. Three days to panic. Three days to flounder.
The rule is prescriptive and must be followed entirely.

By the fourth day, I am fortified. And, so, Daddy shares with
one part regret, one part pride in his accomplishments
of bedding women, sometimes a handful in one weekend,
Daddy's words. Not mine.

Some served with him on neighborhood watch. Some were the mothers of the
PTA.
Daddy was president, a poor man with classical tones resounding from his
long, thick cords like blues from a cello. And, women moved to the sound of
him.

Are some confessions better left unconfessed?

Bed became the verb that broke my mother, but
when a mother forgets her children's names,
what should her children remember for her?

Daddy was the man who met me for lunch at a downtown
deli before, together, we took the D train to Marine Park
to give me my new commute confidence. Later,

we me at college symposiums to hear black intellectuals
dissect the issues. After, we sat for hours to dissect the dissectors.
Then, hugged goodbye. His stubbled cheek to my young face.

Growing older provides perspective. Distance dilutes notions about
what to do with the men.

3.
The question is absurd.

4.
There were four of us girls. I was the baby. The others had me by
eight, ten, and eleven years, so I benefited from my sisters' hair braiding
skills and clothes design. My favorite was the red jumpsuit with shoulder ruffles.
I looked like a five-year-old disco queen the day I wore it for my birthday.
One sister picked my hair out into a globe.

I do not blame any of them for their lack of warning about life in a girl's body,
the ownership some feel to take without permission.
They never spoke of rape by a neighbor or by Nana's boyfriend.

"It's just how it was back then."
I nod. I'm done being a traitor. It is difficult to defend
this place where I enter the story.

Real women grow up and care for the most devastated among us.
I already decided a long time ago, I would be the giver
not the taker of care. Not the interminably wounded. Not my mother.

And, I love a woman, so what does any of this matter to an old dike like me?

Feminine discomfort is too unspeakable.

5.
I know the forces against my man-child.

6.
I must protect him, although I don't know how.

7. The one long gone was the easiest of all.
A stack of papers, a hearing or two, the crack of a gavel,
and it was done.

I did not wish an unnamed relative dead. And each day, I am reminded
I forgive him. And each day, I am reminded, I am the one who is sorry.

8.
I have chosen the path of the giver. Someday, I hope it to be true.
*When Black women are at three times the risk of experiencing a lethal domestic violence than any other racial group.
When the leading cause of death for young Black women between the ages of fifteen and thirty-five is intimate partner violence, and
When the consequence for perpetrators of intimate partner violence is less when the victim is a Black woman

I think of June Jordan's poem about her rights, which is a poem about our rights.

When within weeks of each other,
Brie Golec, a transwoman of color was stabbed by her father, and
Yazmin Vash Payne, a transwoman of color stabbed by her boyfriend, and
Ty Underwood, a transwoman of color shot by her boyfriend

I strain to hear the collective voice of the innocent.

9.

Debbie and I once made soup out of dirt and rain.

*National Institute of Health

As teens, she had Ramell and I—I had an on-again,
off-again thing with Jesus. Between Debbie and Ramell
were Ramell's hands that behaved any which way they pleased,
especially when clenched

My hands secured notes in white envelopes.
"God loves you," my hands
told the pen
to tell the paper
to tell Debbie

No wonder Debbie cut her eyes at me and whispered loud enough for me to
hear her talk about my tired old lady clothes. What else was there to do?
Ramell and I both lost the battle against our powerless hands.
I was an outcast. Ramell and Debbie made a baby.

When Debbie's little brother became a teen
his hand-held heavy steel to the face
of his pretty boo across the street.
When the steel exploded
with one motion of a rogue finger,
little brother's hand brought the steel
to his own face.
However, that time, the rogue finger refused.
It triggered so many questions.

Long before any documents were filed, I recognized
the man I married had the impulses of Ramell
and Debbie's little brother
but the righteous knows what's good.
Race matters.

I know some who speak their innocence
and, are wrongly deemed guilty without due process.

I will shout their cause, but whispering mine would
perhaps cause the earth between us to crumble.

10.

The body becomes inflamed in the protection of itself.
Swelling occurs while questions are held on a very last nerve.

I sit on the floor of my bedroom and in four-square breathing,
I release questions out into the air to revisit at a later date.

Boy child barely knocks. I struggle to my feet. Open the door.
Taller than I am, he lowers his head to my shoulder.
"Goodnight, mom," he says.

In four counts, I release the question and hold him.
Later, I understood, in my arms, was my answer.

The son and the father—Part. 1.

the ohio players set his borough ablaze.
this boy loved a blue rhythm, an earthy funk
distressing this boy's daddy, whose favorite
ditty eased out of a woman from his hometown,
land of the mattaponi, renamed to suit a virgin.

like the first lady of song, this boy's daddy went
to the land of the lenape, lifted by the dutch,
both asylum seekers and southern refugees fleeing
post-reconstruction american apartheid.

this boy's daddy would have told his boy,
"turn that racket down!"
this boy's daddy once tore this boy's earlobe
when he saw a white thread hanging from it,
sewn in with a girlfriend's burnt needle.
this boy's daddy wanted others to see the
light nestled in his boy's afro
and not mistake the boy for being
anything less than a godsend.

this boy's daddy bussed him toward desegregation,
despised apolitical ministers,
and did not fuss with his boy about going to church
but preached into megaphones on behalf of leftists.

this boy's daddy stood between rival gangs,
then guided their searches for an honest wage.
called each one, son. in turn, they called him pops.
this boy knew his daddy was a cool city cat
even though the elder's taste in music leaned sweet
to songs about brown and yellow baskets
and not those smoking riffs that set this boy's borough on fi-yuh.

The son and the father- Part 2.

this father's son is loved.
treasured by the father
and the holy angels, too,
along with a few roughnecks
who step to him on the street
and give him what-up jabs on the shoulder.

i do not mean to compare
this father's son
to the son of the father,
but that is what this father's son
had been to sisters.

one came to him at night
spooked by intracranial jabber.
one saved for him her best jokes.
another came when broken by a boy
the last placed her report card on the table
just before he sat down to eat.
all waited for the flawless response
he was sure to give
as he'd been wisened by the duties
he thought were his.

to sisters
this father's son was close
to the son of the father
when this father/a daddy departed,
not for heaven but for newfound love.

this father's son became a father
before becoming a father.
this father's son
carried a father's weight
because he did not know
who else would carry it.

to sisters,
the one who gabs with the unseen,
the formerly broken, now zealot
the first to die, a comedian,
and especially, the last,
the critic of religious patriarchy,
this father's son,
a shepherd.
and, sisters were lamb.

when the son's father becomes old,
and confusion is a manner of being,
the son's father looks, waits, and asks for his son.

sisters venture to speak but little can be said.
they carry the weight of a father's questions
just as a brother once carried them.

sparrow

she is sitting there
waiting in active, quiet
i wanted to keep you from harm.
you are fluent in her subtleties
even after her death.
no, girl. no. she said
without saying.
when you hold my hand
listen to my pulse
and trust that i know.
but you know she
knows, and none of this has
ever been
about trusting
her.

at fort green park,
well before gentrification,
she tore the wrapper off a pack
cherry lifesavers and offered
one to you, just like in those
old commercials.
you smiled. she half-smiled, again, subtle.
 you wanted to climb the stairs of the
prison ship martyr's monument.
on the first attempt, you stopped less than
midway. looked down.
she was shaking her head, no.
another day, you tried again.
but became engulfed by the sky
that spun as you stood still.
late that summer, the stairs invited you
to try once more. you ran toward them.
"do not think. do not look down.
do not imagine her being afraid for you.
today is the day you will reach the top.
today, you will jump with fists in the air."
after you made it and it

was time to come down,
your balance was uneasy, so you sat
on your bottom and descended by scooting
your behind towards her one step at a time.
she laughed with her belly, shaking
her head with a different tone of voice that said,
girl, you ain't got no kinda sense. her mouth remained
closed, but her meaning was as clear as the
glasses on your narrow face.

even after cremation, her style never changes.
when you find her sitting on
your bed after a long day.
still, without speaking, she tells you
why she is there
*i wanted to prevent you from getting
hurt. I tried.*
"i know," you say to her.
"i felt that. i feel that."
you try to tell her
hurt is only part of you
and that you are capable of
perceiving other parts
because one day, while she held you,
while, perhaps, feeding you,
you locked eyes,
and she never had to say another word.

Juanita

if she had lighter skin, they say
she could have been another brooklyn
starlet, sing stormy weather
like lena horne did in the movies.

she tap-danced in her kitchen, composed
in her living room, spoke
monologues into her gilded bathroom mirror.

what might have been if they hadn't
made us afraid of our goddesses? what if we harnessed
their alchemy to make space for our presence?

when she sang *guantanamera*
a cigar maker, joined the chorus.
and when she strummed her guitar like memphis
minnie, a grandmother, rocked
back and forth the way grandmothers do
when their spirits are stirred.

all principles and heart. sung *time
in a bottle* with sam, her second husband.
time is a question for graying lovers.
never enough time for a woman
whose first husband tried to reduce her
like soup stock. I know how that goes.

being mad took more time than she desired to give
so she wrote about an urgency for peace, though we
were not the ones who initiated war.
but in 1984, she scribbled in "jesse." argued
about the virtues of speaking one's conscience
to those who called it a wasted vote.

Juanita is a starlet now. and it is time
for her dramatic scene. it is quiet
on the set, a recreation
of 1943. she is small-wasted again

and in high heels. she looks
directly into the camera, then up,
when studio rain hits her face.

Goddess of the damned

she be like, damn

She be all tired.
She be like a flattened house shoe.
She be full of compunction.
She be remembering what was said.
She be told what she deserves.
She be believing everybody.
She be weepin' in the bathtub.
She be like her momma,
She be lying.
She be saying it's the arthritis.
She be talking like it ain't her head.
She be actin' like hurt don't bother her.
She be actin' like she foolin' somebody.
She be foolin' no damn body.
She be scattered.
She be slidin' across marbles.
She be grabbin' onto nothin'.
She be almost breakin' her wrists.
She be lying on the floor.
She be holdin' her stomach.
She be trying not to vomit soggy cake
She be wishin' she ate almonds instead.
She be losin'.
She be wantin' rest.
She be told she ain't gettin' shit she wants
and
She be still wantin' shit.

Wind Dream

Nothing here belongs to you.
Nothing responds to the sound of your voice.
Nothing will heed, help, or hold.
Assert yourself. Speak into the
vacancy. Day-old laughter carried
on the pimple of an echo.
Pimple puss drops into your right eye.
Wipe it away and feel it turn to cinder
along with your very own hand

She speaks to wind with a granulating mouth
and pleads with a disappearing throat
in imperfect contrition
she turns into
fine, dry, matter,
embezzled ash
stolen up by greedy gusts.

struggling to form into
something solid, something useful.
defy this force
and become an all-new Super-Friend
who then becomes a wandering albatross

she will not be its burden to bear.
she will spread herself,
all eleven feet of her
clap her bill wildly,
take flight
in search of fissures in the darkness

a breakthrough
to awareness
leaving the brute force of the wind behind.

night perceptions

Sensitivity to cold,
especially the fingertips.
Forty degrees require at least
one layer of fibers.
Soft is best
due to a sensitivity to rough.

Sensitivity to heat
most often at night
under the weighted blanket
due to a sensitivity to defenselessness, a
sensitivity to being unguarded.
In the wee hours, these sensitivities battle,
the one that demands to be cooled
and the one that demands to be swaddled.
They take turns being the victor.
Hour by hour, the weighted blanket
gets dethroned before toppling
its opponent once again.

Then, a memory comes with sudden flashes of light—
a sensitivity to flashes of light
a sensitivity to startling sounds
too loud or too unknown
Which category of storm weeps?
Does it blow in a flat line
or, does it circle and pick up speed?
This sensitivity sweeps them all away.
This sensitivity climbs out of bed and
considers heading for the basement
turns on WCCO and waits until it hushes.

When the only noises heard
are mechanical, motorized, man-made,
a new sensitivity emerges and checks the
front door, then the door to the garage
then sees the red light of the alarm system is on
and goes back to bed.

New rounds of combat come with waves of heat
and the need to be held tight
until the heart finds a good pace.

Then, a new sensitivity consumes her whole,
transmogrifying her into a Neruda poem,
modernista! full of magic
and certain truth
while awake
at the first, second, and third hour.
Can there be a sensitivity to enthusiasm?
At 3 a.m.? Absolutely!

—having her consider galaxies.
the threat of morning
losing its clout to glee,
of all culprits,
asking her to fly under these
conditions—Under these conditions?

She's finally done with suffering fools,
especially the overactive twits
living inside her own mind.

Glee takes up excessive
amounts of space
like the clueless guest
who drinks up your liquor
nothing is funny, but she
laughs anyway and talks too damn loud.

A presence resented by her
and by morning, who will regain
the power to rule her day
to utter ruins.

Her alarm is set to old fashioned telephone
She isn't sensitive to the disruption
as her delta waves slow down.

Soon, she is an old-timey telephone operator,
sleeping on the job.
She sort of hears the ringing until she doesn't.
Sensitivities are so sensitive
they allow her to keep sleeping.

Leave her there. Poor thing, barely got a wink until now.
So what if there is a morning meeting,
she needs rest.

Later, she will confront the sensitivity
to being late and underprepared.
For now, she perceives the world
with a perfect climate for sleeping.

Nerves

I had coffee this morning, so angst is needling out of the center of my chest.
And I feel the laugh/cry sitting heavy at my jawbone, causing it to ache a little.

I just wanted the French vanilla because it smells like sweet rolls
just out of the oven or something else I shouldn't eat while on this journey of

losing. And, with Stevia and plant-based cream,
stone fruit grounds with vanilla bean extract

washed in hot water reminds me of something delicious.

My watery eyes sit open and wild looking. They see such
goodness, like a young Miriam Makeba and Harry Belafonte singing Malaika in a room full of proud black people, but my view is distracted by something tragic that could happen at any moment. Although at this moment, the sun is reflecting off the snow, and the world outside my window is lit like a romantic comedy.

Even still, I might upchuck the coffee and bile churning in my gut.
I have been here before. The first time was twenty years ago. I drank two colas, one behind the other like a big shot. It was the night a hard knock at the door sent me to the ER with a runaway heart, a heart hoarding oxygen and causing me to lose consciousness.

"AVOID CAFFEINE." A recommendation that is easy to forget when I am feeling good about myself because I have exercised for five days straight and ate almost, but not entirely, according to the plan each of those days because I told myself sugar will not overtake me like it did, my sweet, round, gorgeous aunties.

But I am prone to misremembering facts like climate change deniers,
so I drink coffee one day, and I feel fine. I drink it a second day and walk

a mile at lunch and get a lot of shit done, and I'm all impressed with myself
and whatnot. I drink it a third day, and my amygdala turns to slime, oozes out

of my right ear and tickles me as it crawls down the side of my neck and
goes splat on the floor.

I laugh at the thought but then cry again because it would be really bad if that happened. Can't scream it out in the middle of the workday, but maybe I will walk two miles today after eating the salad I packed—But,

what about the fear that I'll be taken up in a funnel? Or that the love of my life will be hurt in a ditch (are there ditches in the city of Minneapolis?) and I won't know where to find her, save her, and bring her back home where she belongs?

When will get my comeuppance for all those I've wronged intentionally or unintentionally because I didn't know or couldn't do any better?

What will I do when I'm invited by the aroma of another something good smelling that will lead me to other dark alleyways covered in glass as broken as my nerves?

no peace

she wanted the iris purple blown glass
and the oversized pillow covered in arsenic-gray burlap.
it was a midday of craving things
that proved the harmony of contrast,
fed a mind designed
to find the order.

once, optimism was her greatest asset.
hope saved her,
so has the fear of looking foolish—
although she violated both instincts
and will again, she is sure.
she returns to her safety
and clings as some cling to
their guns.
she will try to make peace.

but,
something has changed.

who is she in the midst of these battles?
not a deserter, a fighter, a song-and-dance woman
a documentarian, a unifier
not a prophet with knowledge of
how things should end

once she could reason with the other side,
 she had always been able to do the
first knowing
to help others see that contrast works.
"feel the texture of the burlap
that reminds you of wood, somehow,
or a log cabin with an iron stove.
imagine how heavy the stove is.
hold this blown glass in your hands
that could be found in a gallery of modern works.
see this painting; the form of a woman.
carry this newly polished silver

and set it on the rustic
table.
you will see the relation
of things,
and you and I are so much more."
she folds her hands and imagines merging
two brains.

she must find her way into the fight
she did not want,
but has been waged.

reluctant warriors are likely casualties.

Hunger

I been tryna to get you to understand somethin'—
Happiness isn't just handed to most of us. That mess takes work.

Those who are most hungry ain't the ones starvin'
but those who are overfed, who stand too long with the

refrigerator door open tryna decide which piece of
fruit out of a multitude of fruits available to you in this

very moment will be the fruit to satisfy your phantom hunger.
Then, you see the salsa and remember the tortilla chips in the pantry

You wait for it to whisper in your ear—
Yes. You want this acid and salt. You know you do.

But you don't really want that either. And, you think what
you really need is a new job because the one you have

allows you to buy food you ain't got the appetite for, but does not
allow you to drive the car of your dreams. This car you want ain't got a name.

It don't need a name. It just needs to be new—*newer*, as you like to say.
You want a new car, not because the car you drive doesn't

function perfectly fine, or is unsafe. The car you drive doesn't have
that special feature—that automated parallel parking feature.

But you don't really need a car with automated
parallel parking because when was the last time you had

to parallel park?—Well, there was yesterday—
But before yesterday, when was the last time?

In these past two years of Corona, how many times have you
had to parallel park? I bet you can count on one hand.

Or maybe two hands 'cause you had those appointments
at the chiropractor who didn't have a parking lot, and you were

mad you had to find a spot on the street, and you
ended up parking further away than your back could stand.

Your back was aching like a mo' fo. You later realize
you made it worse tryna do office work from the recliner in your living room.
Like the recliner was gonna save you. Make you love your job more.
Only thing it did was wreck your body and take your money

with those appointments that left you with a new injury to your cervical spine.
You tryna be so comfortable you hurt yo' own self.

The last thing you need is a new car, or a new anything.
You didn't even need the new coat you just bought 'cause you were bored

with the perfectly fine coat, you already had.
You said you wanted a bright color to brighten up your winter

As if something you wear on the outside can change everythin' happenin' on the
inside—Just put it on, and voila! Your life doesn't suck anymore

And, anyway, your life doesn't suck at all, chile. You just trifling.
—No. No. That was too harsh. You can just be so sensitive sometimes.

Let's just say, you would be a lot less trifling if you finally got it through your head
that your happiness can't be delivered to your doorstep.

I don't know why you tryna be so happy for anyhow. What's that s'pose to do to
your constitution? Try bein' grateful' for once. Then, you might see this whole mess
turn around.

Goddess of the middle

in the middle i.

first, she asked herself, "am I forty-six, really?"

and wonders if all forty-six-year-olds ask themselves the same question.

four years from fifty. What will the question be then?

ribs, sternum, vertebrae. femur, fibula, hip joint. tibula. her frame.
has carried the flesh of many living beings

a fat baby, a skinny girl, a big woman, a slender woman,
and an even bigger woman

pounds come and evaporate as the sweat dries
and the greens digest.
then come again
and leave slow-
er

either way,

she talks to herself when she walks

hoping the steel fans bolted to the ceiling

do not blow away any poetry
that might escape her mouth

the one who passes her
looks like a fullback
at a really small
private liberal arts college
focusing on musical theater.
his beard does not disguise his youth.
she could be his mother

the second time he passes her
she wonders if that is what he sees,
a mother figure
walking as he runs

though, slightly zanier than
his actual mother
who probably does not
talk to herself in public.

his actual mother might not be
attempting
to art-ify her exercise time.

his actual mother probably
cooked until he was eighteen

so he could grow large enough
for a third-division school
with no athletic scholarships

but he is smart enough
for an elite college of
two-thousand or less
so he plays for the love of sport

like she is learning to do again
at forty-six, she holds herself
together by threads
of the literary kind. Still,
looking for the right words
and accepts the possibility
of never finding them.

in the middle ii.

Her wife sits at her ten-year-old desktop,
translates findings into cohesive language
and makes recommendations.
then stands at podiums and
talk to learners who all want to learn from her.
Her wife desires connection, so she
begins with a few self-deprecating remarks
in exchange for laughter.

This relaxes her, and she is ready to begin.
Her wife is modest, but she is ready
and pleased to be in that enormous space—a darkened
auditorium, the clicker in her hand

When she loses her mother
Her wife kisses her face and rocks her, saying
I will help you in any way I can. And she does.
Her wife buys her a ticket home
so she can sit in front of the golden urn
and bid farewell to what is left of her mother.

Four days later, she is at work.

It is day one of class. She is
an at-will employee
She tells her students her mother has died.
She tells everyone her mother has died.
She is afraid that she may act more strange
than usual.
She hopes others will be forgiving of
her odd behavior
and know her new peculiarities
are probably temporary,
although she has become afraid, they are permanent.
Her wife says she will feel better if
she got work done.
Work is her wife's remedy.
Work works for her wife.

She does not judge her wife.
Work has often worked for her too.

She once worked in a government subsidized high rise
at her mother's kitchen table
covered in decorative plastic.

In high school, she saved history for last
and fell asleep in her textbook.
You work too hard, her mother said
and tried to get her to go to bed.
She got up, washed my face, and sat back down
at the table—
other times, she worked less
She slept away half of a semester in college.
It was her last semester until she returned
three years later to finish.

For many years she worked
at small colleges
encouraging the young who reminded her of herself
to find meaningful work that will sustain them.
Then, helped them stand out, be noticed, get hired
your hard work will pay off, She said.

Her guts were sickly.
Her heart was beating too swiftly.
Her knees unlocked, and she was falling
Work was no cure.
The doctor said, *don't worry. You are not crazy.*
She did not ask if she was crazy.

She wondered if this was her new way of being
stranger than she used to be and
caring less about work.

in the middle iii.

Tall Wife and Less Tall Wife do not vacation often,
They are conservative in their spending
as they prepare for retirement more
than a decade away. They are daughters shaped by mothers who struggled.

So, when the Less Tall wife found herself in that swanky location,
rich tones of gold, bronze, deep chocolates,
and satin sheets, an ornate, three-tiered ceiling
with a chandelier above the bed, she could not bother
to hurry herself, even as they were scheduled
to meet friends at a nearby restaurant.

Less Tall Wife sent the Tall Wife ahead, which was odd.
With all of Less Tall Wife's nervous energy about being with other
people, Less Tall wife's tendency is to arrive early—first,
select the table, make time for steadying her nerves
so that she might be fully present with her company.

However, that time, Tall Wife was ready first, and Less Tall Wife was
lagging behind. *Please start without me. I will be fast*, Less Tall wife said.
She wasn't fast. That luxurious bed seduced Less Tall wife's
tired out, no vacationing bones. She laid across it in her silk nighty
and drifted off until a faint sound outside her window grew louder.
Fire engines. Less Tall wife went to the window and saw the building across the
street was on fire. She panicked but could not move.

Then, the heat on her feet that traveled up to her neck
made her concerned that her building might have
also been on fire. Less Tall wife put on street clothes and
grabbed the doorknob. It, too, was hot. She prayed

Good Lord, help me. This is my worst fear.
The fire safety lesson she had when she was ten said
to shove wet towels under the door and stay put until
you are saved, but she was a black woman.
What are the chances that someone will save her?
So, she bolted.
Less Tall Wife saw fire through the clear glass of the elevator shaft.

She heard people screaming in terror.

She ran down the hall until she saw the door with
the exit sign above it. She walked through it
and entered awakeness,
her real bedroom, not a five-star bedroom.
But if it were a dream, *why the hell am I still on fire?*
Less Tall Wife demanded to know.

She attacked the blankets, ruthlessly kicking them.
Less Tall Wife looked at the Tall Wife, fast asleep in her thick sweatpants
and long sleeves. The Tall Wife's nightwear
allows her to compromise with the Less Tall Wife on the thermostat setting.
Less Tall Wife wonders if Tall Wife will ever experience
night fires,
not that she ever wishes them on her.
Mostly, Less Tall Wife wonders, just how long will she burn.

in the middle iv.

She found herself older than her boss for the first time in decades of work. Theoretically, that is not unusual. v.p. Biden— older than Obama. v.p. Cheney— older than Bush. And this wasn't the first time a younger person had been the boss of her. When she was twelve, and her little sister was four, they both recognized the woman in charge.

In her forties, she realized everyone is on their own trajectory. She understands there are limits to how high she will ascend. She is fond of work where she can sit, ponder, map out, and execute the plan. She enjoys the implementation process. She loves being a resource, being helpful.

She highly doubts if she'll ever steer an entire enterprise. Sometimes she feels some type of way about it. As a whole, black and brown people carry heavy student loan debt due to less generational wealth due and historical shit.

Unlike so many of her queen-boss sisters, she'd rather find a quiet corner to dream than lead a team. Stress has done enough to her central nervous system already, the cortisol levels are already too high. Her medical tests are screaming at her, *Your life expectancy is now in jeopardy!* and she is trying to get a handle on all of it, really. That, alone, is a full-time job. The chronological difference between herself and her future bosses will only continue to grow. Perhaps one of the former students she mentored when they were nineteen and twenty, will eventually sign her paycheck. She decided to be okay with that a while back now. What choice does she have?

Almost a decade ago, she was asked what it meant to her to be an emerging artist at her age. Then, fifty happened, and before she could catch her breath, fifty-two. Clocks be clocking. Doing what clocks do.

She wishes she could say she is standing on the precipices of giving fewer fs—
less fright.
less freeze
less fight...
and, yes, less fucks too.

Her dietician begs her to stop counting and tracking every damn thing.
Stop looking for the perfect mathematical equation. Your body doesn't do math, she says.

Dieticians, these days, are raging against diet culture. She wants to be a badass too.

Stop counting calories, steps, and grams of carbohydrates. Don't measure the weight of your protein, or even the weight of your body. Live your life. Love your life so your body can begin to heal from all of that math you put it through over the span of your entire adulthood.

Subtraction, addition, subtraction, addition. multiplication and exponents have contributed to her state of unwellness.

She stopped feeling ashamed of her plastic plants. Fake foliage is an act of kindness and respect to living philodendrons everywhere. She points it out sometimes when others enter her home. *You see that,* she says, *fake,* and giggles with pride. This, for her, is a step toward self-acceptance.

She has accepted that she is not a climber of the organizational chart. There are other things she desire more.

She has accepted that she is still an emerging artist at "her age."

Just beneath the surface, she is still the little girl who turned to words for comfort. That memory is kept in a locket covered in moonstone, the charm of light, a bringer of clairvoyance.

The moonstone tells her it is the moonstone's job to consider tomorrow and other such matters her hands cannot reach.

Goddess of the integrating lesbian

with no disrespect to officer quinn

they piled into a borrowed, rusted
hatchback. young lives imperil, puttering

across the conduit to queens
to see denzel bare-chested

on a caribbean beach. good girls,
the best kind, supportive and self-determined

known to work too hard sometimes, high
on possibility, sank low and heavy down the coarsely

woven upholstery, holding the same note as a chamber
choir in one voice at the sight of him. she

sat upright, eager only for a safe return to her usual
friday night endeavors, filling pages under a desk lamp,

until Lola, in ginger, showed herself, crooning,
until she could taste the woman's notes.

until she could measure the distance between selves
and the fading crash and a moment of clarity,
and thirty seconds of being self-possessed,

until she could sing along, *I too, like my sugar sweet*
and wonder how on god's perfect earth she could not.

Carried

(for Karyn and Margot)

Laughter tumbles out of an open window,
touches asphalt,
rises and whirls
through the stratosphere.
witnessed by angels.

experienced in moments
curls and falls like iridescent blooms
on a silver lake
twists down pines
and winds its way deep into the ground
anchored in earth
unafraid of muddy boots.

alive like rainwater
falling onto seed
fervent as the foliage you grow
and chop
and stir into iron pots
and scoop generous helpings onto clay dishes
and set on a wooden table
in front of hungry guests.

magnanimous.
    seeks   peace
aligned with the intent to open hearts.
young but
 poised to grow more
exquisite with years.
 a lifetime
lived in moments,
stored in jars
for safe-keeping.

mothers and fathers,
sisters and brothers.

Lift up
affirm
embrace.
elevates this inhabited space.

a conversation
between intelligent women.
egalitarian.

Two whole parts
dreaming,
giving
healing like the apricot tree,
protection under its canopy.

always
joyful laughter from an open window,
spilling   into   everything
buoyed toward heaven

and we are all

carried
        away   with it.

Like You Mean It

Act One

Within our boundaries, a shared understanding between independent forms. Moving in unison with one intention. Amina, perfectly petite with long-legged me heading home. One girl mimick the other girl's stride despite our difference in height. Recapturing the rhythm over and over when one girl falls out of step, confessing our belonging. We belong to one another and this city, but not of this city, like in this world, but not of this world. Amina, breezy, with a girlish giggle, straight teeth, soaring cheekbones, steady on her feet, and nobody's fool. Moody me, mostly agreeable when it is safe to be so.

Otherwise, a girl undercover, pretending to be a wall or a floor. Unmistakably, I was safe and sound in the presence of my sister-friend, Amina, whose Ummi already started her daughter in womanish training: SELF-DISCIPLINE, SELF-PRESERVATION, SELF-REALIZATION, SELF-REGULATION, SELF-KNOWLEDGE, SELF LOVE with Humility, and belief in CommUnity and Obedience to her Higher Power. In the '60s, Amina's Ummi embraced a divine feminine and the verve of the black nation. Mrs. Yusuf gives this to Amina, her daughter. I, through second-hand, grasp as much as I can.

Girls trekked outside of our boundaries and found a park tucked within the topography of concrete, iron, brick, and mortar, under a cacophony of motors, off the riverfront, by the interstate, opposite pier three, behind honeylocusts and planetrees, below grade, down two inclines, the playground Amina and I rediscovered, at twelve, finally, old enough to explore other hoods without supervision. And, this hood was prime property. Its bluffs', its beauty. Girls were in the Heights but not of the Heights, but wished they were for what that would mean. Brownstones. Boutiques. Not diners, but outside dining at eateries with regional menus reviewed and written about in food magazines. Historic doesn't mean old. It means valued. The War Memorial; valued. The Promenade; valued. The visitors; tolerated. The residents; valued and protected from visitors.

We raced to the bottom of the hidden park void of human occupation. No air-sprayed tags, candy wrappers, and cigarette butts. No pigeon poop. No waiting for a kid to be pulled away by hunger or a momma or a friend wanting to hang before being next in line to fly. The seated one taken-up by the one standing. Then, the other girl gets a turn to be the taker-upper, while the seated girl takes a turn at trusting her life to a friend. After years of this, we know we are safe. Brave girls were still smart enough not to soar above the spiked fence. Minding legends of the impaled.

There are no spikes on the playground beneath street level and hidden behind the honeylocusts, and the ground is padded. The parks at home are made for hard heads. A SELF-REVELATION: Outside of our boundaries, I imagine myself a choreographer. Synchronized swinging is the art I will create. Not remembering the aerialists of Ringling Brothers and Barnum and Bailey. Not knowing Canada was in the midst of birthing Cirque Du Soleil. Amina agreed. Yes, a routine. Sit and pump three times, out together, back together. Hop up, perfectly timed. Pump with the right leg. Left leg forward following pointed toes. Keep swinging. Careful. Steady. Fluid motion left leg behind the body as the swing shifts in direction. Timing is bad. Try again. Timing bad. One pumped two instead of three. No. Wrong foot. Try again. First, they ignored the voices of men above. Passersby are hardly worth the attention of girls in the midst of inspired acts.

An imposing voice, low and meaty. *Hey!* We go silent. Then lock eyes. A shout from someone who is pissed, a second voice, refusing to be ignored. *We know you're down there!* Now it's personal. We are off our swings. Men could be heard by the girls but not seen. Girls could be heard by the men but not seen in this park that was just a moment ago a dream. A playground of our own. What were we doing alone, outside of the boundaries of home, trapped at the bottom of a hidden park, without another living soul? If this were a musical, the string section would begin. We reach for each other. Our fates bound. Together. In this, together. *Hey!* That voice again. Harsher now. Loud for that neighborhood. Fully-grown. And male.

Amina, the smaller, me, *Come on!* She whispers. *We can't stay here.*
I'm scared, quivering.
Me too. But trust me. We can't stay here! I trust Amina, so I follow her behind the brick structure—bathrooms, one for boys, one for girls. From a front pocket, a switchblade. From a back pocket, an ice pick. *Which one do you want?* Amina asks.

I never made such a choice before.
I'm scared. Can't answer the simple question. Amina chooses for me, opens the icepick, and places the handle in my hand.

If they come near us, aim for the nuts. Amina demonstrates by jabbing the air. *That's what Ummi says.*

Yes, Ummi. Mrs. Yussuf. She would know what to do, and she put Amina through womanish training so Amina knows what to do. SELF-RESPECT and, most importantly, at this moment in time, SELF-DEFENSE. I wonder why my mother never provided this lesson. My mother's life was full of reasons to provide this lesson.

Come on! Amina pulls my elbow. I imagine taking aim and jamming the pick into a stranger.
Ready?

I run fast, like my friend, up the first ramp. We stand side by side at the bottom of the second ramp. Blocking the exit, two long-haired young men wearing heavy boots and leather. Incongruent with the warmth of the day.

Do you want to hurt us? Amina, the speaker. Her fear, now evident. Switchblade in her dominant hand. I tighten my grip around the wood of my pick, always playing the dutiful student. Always surprised by how little I know.

Delete Act II
Delete the part about meeting the dude with island in his tone
and the way you mistook bookishness for trustworthiness.
Delete the part when you invited yourself to his apartment
<u>SELF-REFLECTION: better left for another day, girl had to run down Utica Avenue alone, remembering her friend's instructions to aim for the nuts.</u>

Act Three
Girls who hold each other's secrets also hold fast to ideas when infestations occur. One could step on a roach and know billions more living in cracks care less about the degree to which they are hated, crawl on their mother's knickknacks and canned peas, lay eggs on their dishes, poop in cold stoves, and wiggle their way inside a baby's ear. Amina and Maribel stomp, mash and whack, spray and place roach gravesites in strategic corners. Lug hate as a tool for the ugly and depraved, certain everyone did the same.

Headline: The long-term health consequence of living in New York City Housing (Politco)

None of us know a scheme was hatched to tilt the globe right. Intelligence looks away from contras because funds are needed to fight socialism. An allegiance made in darkness is the chain to whip the spirit out of potential like Jay. Southern cooking plumped his face rounded him, making him unlike those hard-wired for full-court fast-breaks and finger rolls in midair. Jokester, however, stirs some girls as much as any high-jumping boy. Some try to pull him back to simpler times. He wants this for himself before vanishing under a small mountain made of snow until it thaws.

Headline: Housing Projects Drug Market Born Of Poverty, Neglect (Washington Post)

Tanisha is left without her twin when 8B was set fire. She survives the jump when she lands in a tree. José is shot, and no one snitches. Then, the bodies of the Arnold brothers are found in a luxury high-rise. Prisons increase eightfold, and penny dealers are the first to go. Amina prays to Allah five times a day. I give my life to Christ. Sought protection. Still, we slide onto our bedroom floors at the first pop. The plotters care nothing about girls dropping out of windows, nor do they care for Jay, or José, or the Arnold brothers, who have a few good years with money, before agents keep seized assets for personal delight. Delight. A joy internalized. Energetic madness. Pulling girls forward. Faces fixed beyond our trap when our super predators, our Reagan, Bush, and Clinton era. Our depraved and ugly, our clever beast place gravesites for children in strategic corners.

Headline: "Despite Being the Most Educated, Black Women Earn Less Money at Work, in Entrepreneurship, and in Venture Capital." (Inc. Magazine)

Amina to be a nurse. I, a teacher. It is settled early on, before leaving school, a healthy hood, nourished. A neighborhood read. Children will learn to decipher and critique. Then create their own works. We are a shared belief walking together in unison, demonstrating our belonging to one another. Another lesson in womanishism, SELF-DETERMINATION, also a Kwanzaa thing. Study: an act of resistance. Write the damn paper. Shut down the chick who believes she is the smartest one in the room because she is the loudest one in the room.

Amina and I, our commitment is solid. Are not in it for laughs. And, we squeeze the hell out of each after graduation, *we goin' to college!* Girls proud of themselves, proud of the other. A promise is remembered. Aim, girl. Aim!

After school, girls become women. One moves south, the other west. A decade later, a phone call. Amina a nurse with a kind husband. My life is unfitting, but I am not forthcoming about all of the ways I am unhappy. Change for me is driving with busted tires slapping the road, but change does come as more decades dissipate into fog.

Headline: Owning Your Own Story (Psychology Today)
I marry a good woman, and the two of us are loud and proud in our quiet way. In the comfort of our sweet little house, curled up on a comfy couch, a world to ourselves. In all of this loveliness, I am still prone to profound fears. The sky will twirl. My car will crash or jump a curb. The leaking gas, I swear I smell, will crumble my shelter.

I wonder if my sister-friend from back in the day gets spooked too, and if it has anything to do with the time and place of where our lives began. Then, I remember the weaponry presented to me that day in the park, along with the instructions on how to use it, where to aim. I remember what a mother taught her daughter—all of the ways to hold, love, forgive, believe, and trust herself. The revolution begins with SELF-CARE, along with other instructions. SELF-ASSURANCE has its own tempo. I keep time, and I fall out of step. I capture and lose. Recapture and lose. Stop trying before trying again. Confessing my belonging over and over. A choreographer of memories who will many times lose the beat. Sometimes, strut with SELF-CONFIDENCE.

Overflow

Our feelings are our most genuine paths to knowledge. —Audre Lorde

We feel our feelings.
Feelings form us.
What body can contain the deluge of feelings—
Or, the coming and going and wanting back in
and wanting back out, then in, then out?

Feeling flummoxed
falling apart
Feeling fraught
from the start
Feeling fervor
Feeling growth
Feeling stunted
Feeling both

What is felt when we pretend?
When we feign cool?

Cool cannot be faked.
I tried.

It is the faking that makes me feel flushed.

Fearing not of feelings, completely.
Fear of failing
Fear of flourishing?
Even more, fear of falling out of someone's good graces.
(That's closer.)

Feeling faint and foggy
then fine
then forgetful
then fragile
then fine

—always, always fragmented.

Then, feeling free of the internalized false narratives.
Then, questioning what is false and what is not.

Feeling oh so flawed
then oh so fly

Then, foreshadowing that feeling,
the downward spiral begins with

feeling fair to middling,
frankly, feeling something is unresolved.

Phone a friend
a friendly presence for
friendly banter and
friendly advice
a fruitful chit-chat that is mutually beneficial,
as it should be.

a fresh start to a favorable outcome
a flash of optimism before it fades into murk

Fighting biospheric interlopers of the body
Fighting undifferentiated ghosts. Feeling haunted by the selves.
Fighting selves. Both winning and losing.

Feeling afraid to be forgotten.
What is that   feeling?
Feeling irrelevant????.

From time to time, we suppose
we have felt ir… rel evant too

or like, we have fallen between the cracks.
so says the black child to public education,
so says the black woman to the medical profession

Is there a feeling we have not felt?

for sure…
And we are grateful for it
We are faithful to feeling—no, being decent.

Not pious.

Just not nuclear in scope or shock

Gratitude fertilizes the ground
so that all blossoms may bloom and grow,
Feeling gratified. Gratitude makes us feel enchanted, as in a musical.
Feeling like Lola Fulana
doing high kicks on Broadway
shimmying the perfect shoulders
of a radiant triple threat

There are feelings, on top of feelings, for real

Feeling fatigued by them all.

Then, feeling not too bad.

Then, feeling like the fall guys of our past selves.
What felonies have they committed anyhow?

We feel like we have been framed.
We'd rather be forgotten. Or, forgiven.

We learn we are forgiven.
We are fine.

Fine is fine
but wondrous is better. Feeling wondrous. Feeling like wonders.

Who doesn't feel they are fashioned in the form of the Father?
Fear not. There is Mother.

Feeling elated.
Feeling focused on production. Produce. Produce. Produce. Produce. Produce.

Feeling, in precious moments, nothing.

Feeling like an old stand by
Feeling self-conscious
Feeling awkward.

Afraid of being outed
Afraid of being outside of it all
At times, afraid of being out-numbered

Feelings can be fatal
Feelings should not be dismissed
Feelings should be heard

Speak feeling

Real feelings.

Feel feelings

We are our feelings

Feel me?

Feelers 4 Life. Holla!

Is that pride we are feeling?

Oh, snap!

We are feeling ourselves now!

breath

slapdash wishes fallen onto nearby objects;
a wall, a cooktop, and my plate of dinner.
wishes spoken without hope,
unfulfilled as campaign promises.

order as divine
faith as real as the living ground beneath
this house

god imagined
has slipped through a door
left ajar in my negligence

what keeps me from re-inviting
and resting my cares?
who am I to let go
before securing another
pair of massive hands
to hold my whole world?

dropping vacant wishes onto banisters
and doorknobs and bookshelves
filled with instructions for living

well, i am not. sometimes.
from where is my help?
like breathing in and out,
spirit in thoughtless and thankless
syncopation

then

i remember
it is sunday
and there are
souls that never
needed to be found.
even as a

girl with
sharp elbows
and
narrow calves,

bones
responded
and shifted
weight
as something
unseen
rocked me.

it is sunday and
i won't rise
early in the morning
'cause i am a woman
with too much on her plate.
but when i do rise,
he will not move me.
she will move me.
she knows I may need
late sunday mornings by now.

Writing prompt from Mimi Imuro Van Ausdall: *Write a new word for gender.*

My new word for gender is Blessing.
Who deserves Blessing is yours to name?
Who shall be forgiven are those whom you deem forgiven?
For whom do blessings flow will know for Blessing has and will flow.

Is Blessing new? Yes/And. Blessing has always been.
Has Blessing arrived? Yes/And. Blessing has never departed.
Does blessing have a new name? Yes/And. In this poem, it isn't gender.
It is Blessing's business to be who Blessing be.
It is Blessings business to bless who Blessing blesses.

Goddess of the Integrated Lesbian

You want to deal in salubrious ways.
Listen to Pema Chodron on audiobooks
as you fall asleep. Function out of the body.
Name gratitudes. Go to a church.
Not the kind that puts aches in your ligaments.
Go to Gay Church/
Not Gay affirming,
Gay embodying
aka, a group of queer writers who
are not afraid to use mirth like witch-hazel
for minor afflictions. Not afraid to use the word, Lesbian.
And certainly. Not afraid of the being
who lives over your right shoulder.

You spend time thinking about how the word
triumph is played out. You think of the term *played out.*
And remember that time you were at Debbie Isaac's
birthday party, and you heard her whispering loud
enough for you to hear her talk about your
played-outness—hairstyle, outfit, all-around essence.

You don't know why you believed another girl,
was it Gina who persuaded you? Said, of course, you were invited.
No, you are conflating two prickly events that happened
years apart: Debbie Issac's birthday party when you were eleven
and Gina Clark's baby shower when you were sixteen.

Either way, Debbie Isaac was there for both and whispered
sour nothings about you on both occasions. Had you wondering,
both times, how to sneak out of a circle of girls who would
have been afraid of the word Lesbian.

For a moment, you contemplated trends, and that only
drained you, so you embraced her.
Sometimes embraced her.
Sometimes tried to asphyxiate her.
 Sometimes allowed her to be the shero
she always desires to be.

The one who lives over your shoulder
is all the way *played out.* And so are you.

The two of you. Together. And sometimes you cherish that,
give yourself the biggest, brightest blue ribbon for how
extraordinarily integrated you are! In those moments,
if your therapist issued grades, you would get an A++.

You were once very young and tried hard not to become a victim
of your circumstances—poverty and whatnot, feeling like everything
was your fault, and so forth, and so on. When you are young, and your
dial is naturally set between sad and not that bad, how could anyone
take plain and simple triumph away from you? Who would do such a thing?

When you are older, you know triumph requires acceptance of the
unacceptable or suffer forever. These are the choices.
Choose wrong, and you understand where that saying comes from,
you be doin' too much, too much binging on pacifiers to overcome
sorrows that are meant to be lived with.

You spent much of your life trying not to be *played out* as if
it isn't your default, so afraid of hearing sour nothings being
whispered behind your back, jackhammering yourself into
powdered cement needing to be reset.

You now know, Gay Church will one day affirm this:
Make something of yourself is an unnecessary maxim,
since you already are *something.*
Who knows if you will ever believe this,
even though, at your core,
you can see you *are* the one
who lives over your right shoulder,
and they are a Goddess.

In Gratitude

My wife Buffy is my first reader. I am grateful for her incredible patience and her willingness to read many drafts. Her gut reactions are pure gold. She loved, supported, and challenged me through the completion of this work. I married a Goddess, and life with her is sweet, savory, and deeply satisfying.

My children, Kinsey and Kirby, are also teachers of mine. They are deeply original creative beings who inspire me. My mind is richer because of them. My heart is bigger because of them.

Many who came before me have walked by my side through the writing of this work. I went to the well of Ms. June Jordan many times for guidance and spiritual uplift. In the days we are living, her black, feminist, queer voice speaks deeply into my psyche.

I have been nurtured by many writers who provided feedback, offered encouragement, or served as moral support throughout my writing journey. I give my wholehearted thanks to Carolyn Holbrook, who is magic. She is the mentor who doesn't just offer thoughtful insights. She's been a friend, sister, and advocate providing tangible opportunities for many writers. I will never be able to thank her enough for all that she's done for me over the past couple of decades. Carolyn is also the founder of many, many, groups/organizations designed to assist artists. I have benefited from her service to the community.

Many writers have read parts of this work in various phases. I thank all of the women of Twin Cities Black Women Writing, founded by the wonderful Carolyn Holbrook. I especially thank Carla-Elaine Johnson, who is like a writing doula who invests immense energy in the work of our members. I am grateful for Mary Moore Easter. I gain from her depth of wisdom, poetic skill, and knowledge of the world. TCBWW has provided me with a home not just to share my work but to share my worries and my joy. I'm grateful for the ways we celebrate and motivate one another. All these women have touched me and this work at some stage. Thank you, Telesea Everett, April Gibson, Priscilla Gibson, Lucreshia Grant, Stephanie Chrismon, Davida Kilgore, Arleta Little, Mélina Mangal, Joan Maze, Adobe Okolue, Nneka Onwuzurike, Yvette Pye, LaDonna Redmond, Ashley Richardson, Sagirah Shahid, Hadiya Shire, Erin Sharkey, Princess Titus, and Yvonne Wells-Ellis, Genesia Williams, and Lori Young Williams. I also thank Beverly Cottman and Aundrea Sheppard Morgan, who never really left us, for their gifts remain. There are more

Dear friends who held me together during rough times and celebrated with me in the good times. Palmar Álvarez-Blanco and Derrin Pinto, Elisa Lee, Erica Lee, Marion Goméz, Oyuna Uranchimeg, Janaya Martin, Karyn Cave, Margot Howard, Monica Jarvi, Skyler Jarvi. Thanks to old friends, who remained in my corner even as my life changed in unexpected ways. Thank you, Heidi Koopman, mk Smith, Maggie Kendal, and Ruth Richmond. Thank you, Lakisha Blair and Chanique Ansaar Lewis, for being lights in my formative years that were often dark. Thank you, nurturers of an earlier creative self, Heather Bouwman, Lanay Fjeldahl, Sandie McNeel, Laurel Smith, and Christina Thomsen. So many believed in me and showed their belief in me in very tangible ways, especially when I had difficulty believing in myself. Thank you, Jennifer Dodgeson, Anika Fjardo, Jennifer Kwon Dobbs, Shannon Gibney, Kate Hopper, Lissa Jones, Kate Lucas, Lewis Mundt, Junauda Petrus, Bao Phi, Vanessa Ramos, Sherry Quan Lee, Wendy Roberson, Erin Sharkey, Annette Schiebout, Sun Yung Shin, Satish Jayaraj, David Stein, Peter Stein, Nancy Victorin-Vangeruud, and many others—You gave me a microphone, a stage, a platform, an opportunity, a plug, and I am so grateful! Also, I thank David Mura for his insights about craft from a culturally responsive lens. Those lessons stay with me.

I have deep gratitude for brilliant poet and hardworking art-space maker, LM Brimmer for inviting me to join them in nourishing the Queer Voices of Minnesota community. Our Saturday morning writing circles have also been an incredibly generative space for me. Thank you for the safety we've created together, LM Brimmer, Christian Bardin, Trisha Collopy, Kathryn Hafner, Kara Olsen, Jelani Johnson, Emily Krumberger, Junauda Petrus, Katie Robinson, Taiwana Shambley and Mimi Imuro Van Ausdall and more! Thanks to Hennepin County Libraries. Thanks to the founding curators of Queer Voices, who spent many years holding space for writers like me. Thank you, Andrea Jenkins and John Medeiros.

I also thank other writers with whom I found community during the drafting of this work. Thank you, Fun Fun Cheng, Ting Ting Cheng, Patti Kameya, and Kia Moua. Much of this work was drafted during our time together. Also, thank you, Marisha Chamberlain, Michael Kleber-Diggs, and Kasey Payette, for being early responders in the early draft days. Thank you to Diane Wilson, Rita Pyrillis, Jna Shelomith, Joan Trygg, along with Carolyn Holbrook for the peaceful flow we have found. It is like my writer-self is floating on an easy river.

Thank you to all of my colleagues at MSAB who supported me and stepped in to cover for me when I needed time for creative work or time to recover from various ailments. Special thanks to teammates, Jamie Marshall, Rina Rossi, and Natalie Kennedy-Schuck.

Thank you for making me look good and always bringing so much joy, Anna Min and Tina Cho.

I am blessed to live in a town with the infrastructure to support artistic pursuits. I thank the organizations that have provided me with resources to make work possible. Thank you, Eleanor Savage, for your brave and purposeful leadership and all of the folks at the Jerome Foundation for deepening the work of grantmaking. Thank you, Ron Ragin, with the MAP Fund, for the generous and thoughtful coaching that led to the enormous life changes that were necessary for me. Thank you to the Givens Foundation for African-American Literature, The Loft Literary Center, and the Minnesota State Arts Board. Thank you to the MFA program at Hamline University. Thank you, Patricia Weaver Francisco, Kate Kysar, and Sheila O'Connor. I will always be grateful for SASE: The Write Place and Intermedia Arts, organizations that will always exist in so many hearts.

Thank you, Bea Vue Benson, for the centering guidance that comes from a pure heart, years of experience, and the quest for deep understanding.

Many more have assisted me, encouraged me, inspired me, worked behind the scenes on behalf of artists like me, and offered their kindness to me along the way. My note of gratitude can be a book in itself. Thank you to all of the teachers, friends, mentors, loved ones, and those who support me from near and far distances.

I thank my family of origin. I thank my beloved mother, Doroththy Fernandez Williams, who watches me from the spirit land and reminds me still to stay safe. I thank my father and cheerleader, Herbert Williams. My parents knew I was capable of finding my way. I'm still trying to see what they saw. I thank all of my siblings, Anthony, Eric, Herbie, Jeannie, Patricia, and Shariece. As well as the sister and brother who transitioned some time ago, Tina, and Victor. A lot of it wasn't easy and still ain't.

Last but not least, it is essential that I thank the ancestors for surviving the worst and having hope to believe there was a future. Some may want us to forget the atrocities. We never will.

Other versions of the following pieces were previously published :

Crave, she be like damn, and there is no simple answer, previously published in *Wrath-bearing Tree*

The Crossing, previously published in *Aquifer: The Florida Review*

how she keeps, previously published in *New Limestone Review*, University of Kentucky.

Homeland, Like the Girl who Sang Soweto, after June Jordan, previously published in the anthology, *Can't Stop, Won't Stop: Poems in the Wake of Racial Injustice*, edited by Mary Moore Easter

Hunger, previously published in *Dillydoun Review*

Like You Mean It, translated into Spanish by Laura Corcuera and published in *Pequeñ tratado de amistad: Hacia una politica de respeto*, an anthology edited by Palmar Álvarez-Blanco

May the Circle, previously published in the *minnesota review*, Duke University Press

Sherrie Fernandez-Williams earned her MFA in Writing from Hamline University. She is a 2021-2023 Jerome Hill Artist Fellow and a 2021 Black Voices in Children's Literature winner. She received an Artist Initiative Award through the Minnesota State Arts Board, a Beyond the Pure Fellowship, a SASE/Jerome Grant, a Jones' Commission Award through the Playwrights' Center, a Givens Black Writers Collaborative Fellowship, and was a Loft Mentor Series Winner in Creative Nonfiction. Author of *Soft: A Memoir*, Fernandez-Williams has published poems in journals including New Limestone Review, Aquifer: The Florida Review, and Duke University Press, among others. Her essays can be found in the anthologies including, *We are Meant to Rise: Voices for Justice from Minneapolis to the World, Can't Stop Won't Stop: Poems in the wake of racial injustice, How Dare we Write: A Multicultural Creative Writing Discourse* and *The Poverty and Education Reader*. She co-curates the Queer Voices Reading Series with LM Brimmer in collaboration with Quatrefoil Library and Hennepin County Libraries in Minnesota.

Printed in the USA
CPSIA information can be obtained
at www.ICGtesting.com
JSHW082051290723
45531JS00002B/15